Also by William Claxton

Jazzseen

Claxography: The Art of Jazz Photography

Jazz: William Claxton

The Rudi Gernreich Book

Jazz West Coast: The Art of the Record Cover

California Cool

Pictures of Peace

Jazzlife

LAUGH

Portraits of the Greatest Comedians and the Funny Stories They Tell Each Other

Photographs by William Claxton

Introduction by John Lithgow

Conceived and produced by Andy Gould
and Kathleen Bywater

Text edited by Mike Thomas

William Morrow and Company, Inc.

New York

It is the policy of William Morrow and Company, Inc., and its imprints and affiliates, recognizing the importance of preserving what has been written, to print the books we publish on acid-free paper, and we exert our best efforts to that end.

Library of Congress Cataloging-in-Publication Data
Claxton, William.
    Laugh : portraits of the greatest comedians and the stories they tell each other / William Claxton ; text edited by Mike Thomas.—1st ed.
        p. cm.
    ISBN 0-688-15891-9
    1. Comedians—Portraits. 2. Comedians—Anecdotes. I. Title.
PN2285.C52   1999
792.7´028´092273—dc21   99-19846
                            CIP

Printed in the United States of America
First Edition

1 2 3 4 5 6 7 8 9 10

BOOK DESIGN BY SISCO & EVANS

www.williammorrow.com

Acknowledgments

Books like this take intense hard work, and *Laugh* could not have been completed without the support of all the great comedians, comedic actors, and comedic writers: Liz Ryan, my friend and associate; William Claxton, Bob Zmuda, and Mike Miller from *Comic Relief*; Paul Fedorko; Denise Abbott, who conducted the initial interviews and worked on the initial text; Mike Thomas; makeup stylist Richard Bernal; William Morrow Senior Editor Doris Cooper, and her assistant Kelli Martin; Alan Nevins, our literary agent at Renaissance; and the Beverly Hilton Hotel.

I would also like to thank Geoff Bywater, who inspires me in all ways; Julia, Geoffrey, Grace, and David Bywater, my four lovely children; David Turner, my guiding light, and Raymond, Mary, Kevin, and Vivian Turner, and Mark Beaven for keeping the entrepreneurial spirit alive. Finally, thank you to my great friends, Barb Bittner, Mapy Locker, Teri Horner, Pam Ferguson, and Joey Lynch.
—*Kathleen Bywater*

First and foremost, I want to thank the comedians, without whom there would be no book. I would also like to thank William Claxton for being a gentleman and a wonderful talent. And Alan Nevins, Jodie Wilson, Rob Zombie and Sheri (for sharing my humor), Terry—my brother, all the guys in my office, especially Rob McDermott and Barbara Rose, Walter O'Brien (for always laughing at my jokes), Natalie Anderson, and Georgia Archer for introducing me to William Claxton. Lastly, to Sid and Vi, my parents, whose laughter always got me through and still does!
—*Andy Gould*

Andy Gould had the idea and vision for a book called *Laugh*. Without him there would be no book. Another thanks for Andy for asking me to photograph these great comedic artists.

Thank you to Kathleen Bywater and Liz Ryan for tracking down these busy actors. Not an easy feat. Thank you Steve Crist, my friend and associate; Don Weinstein and his staff at Photo Impact; Richard Bernal, groomer and makeup man extraordinaire; Ara Nuyujukian and Samantha K. Corn of Eastman Kodak Professional; Peter Bradshaw of ProFoto AB of Stockholm; and Mamiya America Corporation. My Mamiya 645 ProTL camera and lenses were used throughout this project. And special thanks to Doris Cooper, our editor.

—*William Claxton*

Contents

Introduction

I can't remember how or why I was picked. Maybe there was a general consensus. Maybe I was the obvious choice.

However it happened, I was cast as the damsel in distress in the big outdoor show that ended our week-long Boy Scout Camporee in the summer of 1956, somewhere in the dark woods of Ohio. I was eleven at the time.

The show was a travesty of the old melodrama where the villain ties the heroine to the railroad tracks, only to have her be rescued by "her hero." We were to perform without rehearsal, throwing ourselves on the mercy of three hundred jeering scouts. Before my entrance, I stood in the darkness waiting to go on. Barelegged and shod in hiking boots, a shirt around my middle for a skirt, and a bandana around my head for a bonnet, I was shaking with fear and sick with impending humiliation. Not only was I about to make a horrible fool of myself, but my eleven-year-old masculine ego was in dire jeopardy.

You can guess the payoff. I killed. My damsel in distress was greeted with gales of Boy Scout laughter; my exit in the arms of Eagle Scout Larry Fogg elicited deafening cheers. For months afterward I was the star of Troop 68. In one clumsy five-minute skit, I had been snakebit by comedy. I've played dozens of comic roles since then, and perhaps it's no coincidence that four or five of them have been performed in drag.

My point? Every soul whose mug appears in this volume could describe a snake-bite moment like mine. We have all had a first time, when, often unwittingly, we unleashed a torrent of laughter from an audience, changing our lives forever.

That moment is often a complicated one. Remember how scared I was? How queasy? Remember the jeopardy? The fear of humiliation? The fragile male ego? The intensity of those feelings surely account for the equally ecstatic release that a performer experiences when an audience laughs out loud. This curious tension between insecurity and audacity is something that every comedian and comic actor knows in his or her bones. It is what makes the following words and pictures so fascinating.

William Claxton understands this duality. Although he is a man with a winning sense of humor, Claxton is also an artist of high seriousness. The first time I met him was in a setting far removed from laughing crowds. He'd been assigned to do special photography for the film *Then There Were Giants*, which I was working on, in Prague, Czech Republic. Presumably he'd drawn this assignment because his photographer's eye suited the film's darkly serious themes.

Look at his portraits of these fifty funny men and women. Their faces will delight you and remind you of a thousand jokes and sight gags. But look behind their eyes. You know they love to get laughs, but why do they do it? Why do they want it? Why do they need it? And when did they discover that love, want, and need? You sense that Claxton was intrigued with these questions himself, and that he used his camera to seek the answers.

Nowadays I play the high commander on a sublimely ridiculous sitcom, *3rd Rock from the Sun*. In the first year of its run, my birthday arrived and my producers presented me with a wonderful gift. It was a framed photograph of Noel Coward, sitting at a makeup table in an evening dress, his jaw resting jauntily on his fist. The photo has hung on my dressing room wall ever since. It always makes me smile, even though it radiates ruefulness and melancholy. For me, that one image sums up what is delightful, complex, and challenging about comedy. It was taken by William Claxton.

So can you imagine the thrill on being asked to appear in this volume? "Claxton will photograph me?" I asked incredulously. "I'll appear alongside Rickles? Burnett? Conway? Cleese? Williams?" I thought someone was joking. But then I remembered the summer of '56 and thought that, yes, perhaps I belonged in their company after all.

—*John Lithgow*

LAUGH

At age five,
my youngest son, Cody, is already a chip off the old block.

He even does stand-up routines. He sprang this one on me recently:

"Knock, knock."

"Who's there?"

"Peanut butter."

"Peanut butter who?"

"Peanut butter and jelly."

I never said he was a pro. When I don't laugh, he taps his fist on the table, pretending it's a microphone. "Is this thing on? These are the jokes, folks." When I actually *tell* him, "That's just not funny, Cody," he's got his heckler comeback down pat: "Hey, I don't bother you when you're working at Burger King!"

What a kid. They grow up so fast. Next thing I know, he'll be playing the Met. But until then, the hat stays in storage.

Robin Williams

For one brief,

shining moment, I was a strung-out lesbian pinko.

It was the summer of '77 and I was reading water meters for the city of Marietta, Alabama, a gig no less exhilarating than shucking clams. Needless to say, I was goddamned sick of the mind-numbing monotony. And maybe crazy from the heat, too, because I decided to enlist in the United States Army—Bulldozer Repair Division, both of which, unbeknownst to me, had a surplus of loose screws.

But on my first day of duty, I had a sudden change of heart (read: burst of sanity) and politely informed my recruiting officer, a surly, burly slab of an ape who got off on shattering eardrums, that I had no future in heavy machinery, and that I wanted out. *Now.* With the air of southern gentility for which Alabamians are known, he explained that this was impossible seeing as *"We own your sorry ass!"* Then he fetched more surly, burly men like himself, and together with his Neanderthal platoon, began barking more dumb-ass clichés from the army handbook until I could take it no more. "Look," I cooed, ever the model of grace under fire, "if I have to fly a hammer-and-sickle flag, stick a needle in my arm, and start eating pussy, I will!"

I was discharged that very day. Which just goes to show that in This Man's Army, you can't have your pussy and eat it, too. Or something like that.

Brett Butler

Looking back

nearly a quarter of a century later, perhaps

one afternoon of horror was indeed the funniest, most surreal moment I've ever had onstage as a comedian.

Only in the business for a couple of years, the good news was that I was the opening act for a Sonny and Cher tour. The bad news was that not only was I unknown to most of the audiences, but the shows were usually in front of more than ten thousand people, night after terrifying night.

This particular gig was at a state fair. Let me cut to the hilarious, gruesome details. The show was at two o'clock in the afternoon. The stage was at one end of a race track in the middle of the fairgrounds, with a grandstand of thousands of Sonny and Cher

fanatics easily a quarter of a mile away. Looming behind the stage was the frightfully close roller coaster, from which the screams of delighted riders yelped every seventeen seconds as they headed down the final plunge. On the stage dressed in a black suit (which probably made me look like nothing more than a little Jewish bowling ball, from the vantage point of the audience), I was just a few feet away from gigantic speakers, which made it impossible for me to even hear myself worry, let alone remember my act. These speakers were easily twenty feet tall and five feet wide and their only positive use was that they allowed a good buddy of mine, who came to the show with me, to hide behind one of them and shout out words of encouragement and (toward the end of the show) other possible careers.

To make matters worse, I had to do exactly thirty minutes! No more, no less. The front of the stage, I think it bears repeating, was so far from the crowd that I felt I was performing in a neighboring state. In case I didn't go over, while I was on, the promoter thought it wise to parade "animal oddities from the circus world" across the stage. Their sad-looking physical disappointments brought "oohs" and "aahs" from delighted ticket holders.

So there I was, having the good fortune to be on the bill with this celebrated super-duo, yet forced to look down at camels with five humps, depressed seals who couldn't balance balls on their noses, zebras with polka dots rather than stripes, sobbing hyenas, and an endless variety of freaky curiosities.

To say I bombed would be bad reporting. It's hard to know what happened because it ended so fast. At that time in my career I pretty much knew the sequence of my routines, and it's not uncommon for young performers like myself (at the time) to race through the act if the crowd isn't with you. In this case not only was the crowd not with me, but they were so far away, even if they had laughed I could only have heard it through word of mouth. So with the roller coaster drowning out my pain and the animals amusing the onlookers, I raced through a thirty-minute set in a little under four minutes, grabbed my friend, and ran for my life. I figured my career was over.

Out of harm's way and well beyond the grandstand, I sat shaking as I told my buddy I was curious to see how Sonny and Cher would handle this situation. Well, they turned their usual ninety-minute show into something like twelve minutes and got off.

I was ecstatic! They bombed, too! So it seemed. I mean, I dug them, but hey, I felt like shit, and misery loves company. Yet as it turned out, I found out that most everybody sucks at venues like this, and the fact that I did too only made me feel more a part of show business than ever before! I was going to be star!

Richard Lewis

Adolf Hitler

and my cat Sylvester were separated at birth.

Aside from sporting a similar mustache, the two shared a common bond: they were loathsome, evil pricks.

The Hitler resemblance aside, Sylvester was unlike any being on the planet, including his fellow felines. As we all know, most cats will rub up against just about any warm body in close proximity. Not Sylvester. He'd do so only against women. For which who could really blame him? Still, it's emasculating to be snubbed by your pet, especially one that licks his own privates. For which who could really blame him? "Hi, Sylvester," I'd say, trying to get his attention. But he'd just hiss and walk on past. Furry ingrate.

This went on for years until one day, I got fed up. That's it, I declared, thoroughly disgusted. I cook for you, I clean for you, I put a roof over you, and you don't even have the common courtesy to rub up against my leg. I'll show you who's boss around here.

So I went into the other room and put on my wife's hairpiece, negligee, and sunglasses. Only Abe Vigoda in a thong would have been sexier. "Hello," I called out in a high-pitched voice. "It's Auntie Mame. My, what a *beautiful* apartment you have! And my, what a *pretty, pretty* pussy cat!"

Well, that was all the prodding Sylvester needed. In a flash, he was humping my gams and purring with delight. Gotcha, ya little bastard, I thought, carrying him into the bedroom, where our lovemaking session intensified. "You're a sweet kitty. Yes you are," I purred as I lay with him on the bed, stroking him ever so gently. Soon, his moans of ecstasy reached a feverish pitch. Ha! My plan was working. Sylvester was totally lost in the moment.

Then, without warning, I ripped off the wig and shades. Sweet Moses! Auntie Mame was a *man*! God, did that cat shriek. He flipped ten feet into the air and scrambled beneath the bed. Or, he tried. He couldn't quite squeeze his overfed ass under the frame. I just sat there, laughing hysterically, proud of myself for having outsmarted a dumb cat. Okay, so it was a slow day. But at least Sylvester knew who wore the pants in that house, I reasoned, adjusting my nightie.

Charlie Callas

s hasn't

minished the deep respect
I have for my predecessors,

guys like Jerry Lewis, Buddy Hackett, Alan King, Richard Belzer—comics whose collective aroma is not unlike that of the Stage Deli: corned beef, rare.

About six years ago, when I was fairly new to the business, those idols of mine, the ones I just mentioned, showed up at the Friar's Club Comedy Festival in New York City. I nearly orgasmed when I saw them there. It was largely because of them that I'd become a comic in the first place. So, eager to introduce myself, I weaseled my way backstage.

I was among giants here, and feeling really out of place. I tried desperately to blend in, but I still looked like a groupie. What am I saying? I *was* a groupie. So I lurked in the shadows and schemed. How would I approach them? Next thing I knew, they approached me. This was the break I'd been waiting for. Though the only thing they were waiting for, I noticed, was the elevator, next to which I was standing. To the casual observer, it probably looked as though I were a member of this comedic rat pack. In reality, I might as well have been a panhandler.

If I couldn't join them, I decided, I'd eavesdrop. So I pricked my ears and hunkered close. Jerry was nearing the end of a story he'd begun earlier, something about a recent event he'd attended. " . . . and people were packed so tight, you couldn't do *this* without hitting somebody," he exclaimed. And as he uttered the word *this*, his fist lashed out and accidentally drilled me in the sternum. I went down for the count.

To add insult to injury—really, it hurt— no one seemed to care that I'd been knocked on my ass. I mean, who'd have thought he could throw like that? While a part of me felt strangely honored to have been slugged by the King of Comedy, the rest of me felt like spit—in a humorous sort of way. No "Sorry kid." No "Let me help you up." They just continued their conversation as if nothing had happened.

I was still on the floor when the elevator arrived. From my wormlike vantage point, I watched them board, and as the doors began to close, I heard one of them ask, "So, Jerry, you seen Dean lately?"

You're nobody till somebody loves you.

Jon Stewart

Some years ago,
my husband and I rented a house
in the lovely

Kensington area of London, England, where I was filming a television show. The morning after we arrived I took tea on the terrace. How British of me. Glancing out on the neighborhood, I was struck by one of the funniest, most bizarre sights I've ever seen: a herd of horses sunning themselves on the top-story balcony of the high-rise across the way. Apparently, manure-covered hay wasn't good enough for them. Nonetheless, while I knew the Brits were quite proper, this seemed ridiculous! Even my British husband couldn't make sense of it.

Though, as we later learned, these weren't just any horses, they were the Queen's horses, and she housed them in this equines-only apartment building, where they were pampered until Her Majesty wished to enlist their services for the occasional royal outing.

I almost envied them. What a great life, not to mention a great subject for the Discovery Channel: "Idle Rich of the Animal Kingdom." A ratings blockbuster, I'm sure.

Rita Rudner

to Bob Fuckin' Hope's page. Oh, I guess he's not in here. But you get what I'm saying, right?

It's just that people always peg me as a "comedian," and I'm NOT A FUCKING COMEDIAN! *GOD!* I don't have funny shit about my relatives or my dog or my car. That stuff's fuckin' pedestrian. Oh, sure, I'm on a nice little prime-time sitcom, *NewsRadio.* But you know what? I've played a lukewarm pussy fag on that show for five years now, and it's old hat. I'd much rather be onstage, shaking it up. I'm sick of being Mr. Fuckin' Goofy.

Although goofy sells, I know. I know because industry people always tell me, "Turn up that goofy meter, Andy!" No, I want to say, I'm gonna turn that fuckin' goofy meter *OFF.* Better yet, I'll fuckin' break that fuckin' goofy meter over your fuckin' head! Fuckin'

comedy album, and I'm like, "Guys, I want to make fuckin' MUSIC here. *HOT FUCKIN' MUSIC!* I want this album to be HOT! *HOT FUCKIN' SEXY FUCKIN' HOT FUCKIN' SEXY FUCK HOT SEXY FUCK FUCK FUCK!"* Eventually, they caught on.

So anyway, I'm sorry I can't provide you with a ditty that makes me laugh. Truth is, I'd rather disembowel myself with a spoon. Really, I don't even know what the fuck I'm doing in this book. Whatever.

Rainbow Prod

Andy Dick

You know,
I like to consider myself a clever man.

A not-unwitty man. A person who appreciates sophistication, subtlety, and nuance. And yet, I must admit that to me, nothing is funnier than a person getting hit on the head. Not to the point of injury, of course. But a nice thwack to the back of the skull? Nothing funnier. If it makes a funny noise, even better. And I'm not a purist about it; the bump can be accidental, deliberate, to the back, to the front, to the side of the head—I just enjoy them all.

All right, so now you know.

Paul Reiser

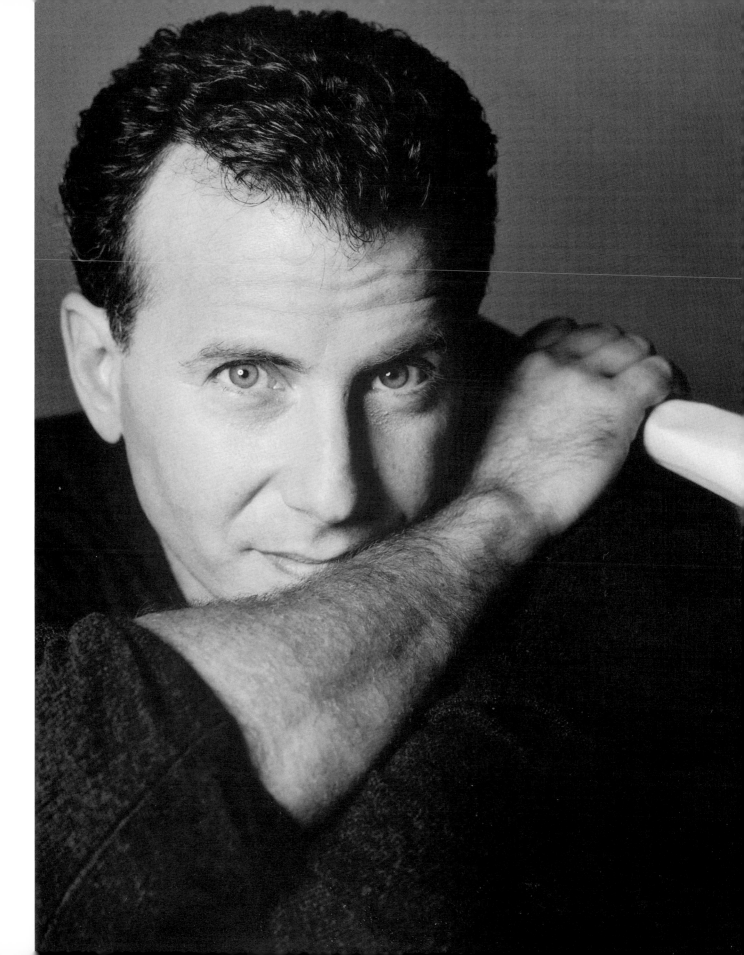

I have not

one iota of musical talent.

It is a bane of my existence that I will, I fear, bear forever. As early as age ten, my piss-poor pitch was apparent. I was, I recall, expelled from singing class and told instead to occupy the hour with extra Greek. Just what I needed, more Greek, the language of international diplomacy. To this day, I've barely uttered a word of the tongue, except to cuss out a waiter who nearly incinerated me with a plate of flaming cheese.

As the years passed, I became quite an accomplished actor; my vocal shortcomings no longer troubled me as they once had. Until, in 1964, I was asked to audition for *Half a Sixpence,* a Broadway musical. Shuddering at the thought, I nonetheless obliged, not thinking for a second that I would actually be cast.

At the audition, the producers asked me to sing, of course. This was, after all, a *musical*. I don't know any tunes, I lied, trying desperately to avoid humiliation. Then just sing your national anthem, they replied. Further ignominy. I truly *didn't* know the words to that. So they fed me the lyrics, which I sang atrociously. Then I went happily home, certain I'd sufficiently conveyed my melodic ineptitude.

I was wrong. They offered me the role, apparently because I'd made them laugh during dialogue scenes. Cursed comedic genius! So the next day, I spent a few minutes warbling at the piano with the late Stanley Lebowski, a famous Broadway director, who wore an increasingly pained expression with each note I belched. Upon recovering, he simply said, "John, just mime."

Which was fine with me. Still, I had to learn the words to all the musical numbers so as to fake out the audience. But I never uttered a peep. For the first six weeks of the run, that is. After fifty or so performances, I felt quite comfortable with the role and so began, softly, to join in with the chorus.

A few days later, I emerged from my dressing room to see Lebowski scowling at me from the corridor. "John," he snarled, "are you *singing*?"

"Only a bit, Stan," I replied sheepishly, amazed he'd heard me amidst a sea of booming voices.

"Well, *don't*!"

John Cleese

Nude pygmies

notwithstanding, *National Geographic* television specials

have taught kids a great deal about nature. But as I've learned, that's not always a good thing.

One afternoon, when my son Cooper was about two, we sat watching a special on birds. Cooper's eyes would widen every time the camera zoomed in on wise old Mr. Owl, perched gargoyle-like in a tree.

"What sound does Mr. Owl make?" I quizzed.

"Hoo! Hoo!" Cooper replied, blissfully beaming. What a sweet kid, I thought, thankful he'd be sheltered from life's ugliness for a good while longer.

At which point Mr. Owl swooped down, snatched up an adorable little field mouse, tore off its head, and swallowed it whole.

"Daddy," said Cooper, innocence freshly marred, "I'm hungry for meat."

Thank God *Alien* was on past his bedtime.

Rick Reynolds

By most
standards, I'm a good-looking guy.

By most *normal* standards, that is. When I used to go on commercial auditions, I felt like a troll. It'd be me, and this roomful of Greek sculptures. God, they were handsome.

The one consolation was that none of them had a single funny bone; they were all so absurdly serious. Hey, guy, I thought at one audition in particular, it's a commercial. Get a grip. Amid the virtual silence, I looked around and saw all these beautiful heads buried in the "script" du jour. The whole room was deep in concentration. I knew this because many tongues were sticking out, a sure sign. I think Einstein used to do that while he was devising his theory of relativity.

But despite the fact that I was, undoubtedly, the funniest guy in the room, I still felt like Quasimodo among these chiseled specimens. Look away! I'm hideous! I just wanted to do my shtick and get the hell out of there. What time was it anyway? I wondered, glancing at the wall. What's this? Three clocks? How useless, especially since one of them was set to U.S. time. The other two were set to Rome and Tokyo times, as if someone would suddenly burst into the room and exclaim,

"Oh, shit! What time is it in Rome? I'm late for an audition!"

Speaking of which, I bombed mine horribly. At which point I decided that rather than write off the entire day as a bust, I'd have a little fun, fuck with my beautiful brethren. It was my duty as a comedian, I reasoned, to put some levity in their lives. So on my way out of the audition, I dramatically threw open the reception area door, burst into the room, and, panic-stricken, yelled, "Oh, shit! What time is it in Paris? I'm late for an audition!"

Silence. Blank stares. Tongues frozen in mid-thought.

"Come on, people! No Paris clock, get it?" Nothing.

Though the gag bombed horribly, I remained assured of my comedic superiority. But even that consoled me less with each passing second. As much as I didn't want to admit it, I knew it didn't matter whether they "got it" or not. As I stared at them and they at me, one thought kept pelting my brain: God, they were handsome.

John Henson

As a writer

language is my greatest ally
and worst enemy.

Evidence of the latter: Some years ago, while vacationing in Kauai with my then-girlfriend, Lyn, I found myself hopelessly tongue-tied. It was late afternoon, and the tropical rain was hypnotic. I should have been relaxing, taking it all in, but my stomach was in knots. You see, I was on the verge of proposing to Lyn, who lay nearby in a hammock, lulled to listlessness by the balmy breeze. She'd reached her happy place, and I knew I shouldn't rouse her.

But I couldn't help it. I had to tell her how I felt, that I wished to spend my life with her, that we were kindred spirits. I stood speechless, my usually brimming arsenal of bons mots utterly depleted, when suddenly, earnestly, in her general direction I blurted, "How can I show you?" Then, crescendoing, *"How can I tell you?"* *"WHAT CAN I DO?!"* My pleas took on feverish fervor.

For a moment there, I hoped she hadn't heard me. But of course she had. And when my love stirred, this was her reply, murmured ever so sweetly, if a bit sleepily: "You can leave me the fuck alone."

I've always envied her way with words.

Norman Lear

Even now

having seen what I saw—
the chaos, the carnage,

the blithe denial—I still regard my father
as the world's most even-keeled man.
Everything about him is balanced, calculated.
Ask him about his lawn, which he mows
weekly without fail, and he'll wax
philosophic. Tell him to dress up, and he'll
don his best suit, which is, in fact, his only
suit. And it doesn't take much to impress him.
Once, I gave him a nose-hair trimmer for
Christmas, though by his reaction you'd have
thought it was a Ferrari. Nonetheless, the
utter sanity of his life has been known to go
AWOL from time to time, as it did one fateful
day long ago.

I was home on hiatus from *Saturday Night
Live,* and Dad and I made a trek to the
grocery store. Great, I thought, a little
bonding time with the Old Man. So there we
were, just the two of us, strolling down the
paper goods aisle, chatting manly chat, as
fathers and sons are wont to do, when he just
snapped.

What possessed him, I'll never know.
A synaptic misfire, expired milk, Gozer the
Gozarian. Whatever it was swept over him
like an evil tsunami. In an instant, he became
this raving loon as one after another, he
began firing rolls of toilet paper across the
aisles. His aim was indiscriminate. It didn't
matter who stood in the line of fire. He was
shooting to kill. God would sort them out.

And then, just as suddenly as this TP
offensive had begun, it was over, and he
sauntered on his merry way, as if nothing had
happened. Though I sensed from the impish
twinkle in his eyes that he took perverse
pleasure in the havoc he'd wreaked.

Dan Aykroyd

As youths,

my daughters could
be quite the little hellions.

They'd alternate moody days so never once were all three simultaneously cheerful. Which, as you can imagine, made for some lovely family outings.

Years ago, my husband and I schlepped the tots to dinner at a favorite L.A. restaurant. The gods, it appeared, were happy that night, because both Carrie and Jodie were simply angelic. At the same time. Glory be! And then there was my youngest, Erin, the evening's wild card. It was, I soon realized, her turn to piss off Mommy.

When the waiter arrived to take our orders, my ballsy tyke decreed, "Just dessert, please." Never one to brook guff from my precocious progeny, I sternly informed her in no uncertain terms, "No dinner, no dessert." "Fine," she shot back, "then I won't eat!" Meanwhile, her older sisters must have spotted my steely gaze and decided it would be best to stay on their mother's good side tonight. "More broccoli and carrots and salad, please!" they pleaded loudly, attempting to slather the matronly ass as best they could.

But I paid little attention, as I was too busy glowering at my youngest child, who glowered right back. Stubbornly, both of us refused to lose face, and so the ridiculous standoff continued throughout the entire meal.

At last, Erin broke down, as kids will often do when properly intimidated. "Daddy," she chirped, turning to her father, batting her lids, "I love you." Then, nervously, she added, "And, Daddy, I also love your wife."

Carol Burnett

The early days

of my stand-up career were filled with shitty one-nighters,

some of the worst of which were in or around Boston. One time, I was booked at this biker joint called Jimmy's in Dedham, Massachusetts. It was the kind of place where the "stage" was nothing more than a tiny, slightly elevated nook right next to the bar. No walls, nothing. Just a few fold-out chairs and a puny state-of-the-art Radio Shack sound system—a fucking Mr. Microphone, basically.

Late in the evening, after most of the patrons were sufficiently sauced, the bartender flicked off the hockey game and told everyone it was "comedy time!" Oh, joy. Predictably, most of them just ignored him and kept right on yelling and drinking and being real obnoxious in general. I wasn't about to tell everyone to shut up and listen (mostly because I wasn't in the mood to get my face kicked in). So I thought, fuck 'em, and began my act anyway.

A few minutes into the set, as I was attempting to interact with the "audience," I spotted this beefy biker dude stumbling toward the stage. And he wasn't just drunk, he was fucking plowed. I mean, his eyes were little slits—he could hardly see. "Aw, shit," I heard people say in slurred Bostonian

accents. "Aw, fuck, heah comes Johnny. Aw, shit, that comedian guy, he's fucked." One look at Johnny and I figured that out for myself. But there really wasn't much I could do. There was nowhere to hide, and I was pretty sure that despite Johnny's visual impairment, he'd crush me if I tried to escape.

When he finally staggered up beside me, I caught a whiff of his nauseating aroma— beer and pit with a hint of ass. Trying not to panic (or vomit), I playfully announced, "Heeeeere's Johnny!" Then, I held out the microphone, reporter-style, and asked him, "So, what do you have to say, Johnny?" But Johnny didn't want to talk. Which became immediately apparent when he snatched me up in a bear hug and began licking my head. Teeth, eyes, cheeks—everything. He slathered me good, Johnny did.

All the while, the mic, sandwiched between my face and his hulking frame, picked up Johnny's nasty slurping sounds and broadcast them for all to enjoy. And, boy, did they enjoy. By this point, everyone was laughing and pointing because, hey, it's funny to watch a slight, bespectacled, balding guy get molested by the slimy tongue of some reeky-ass, fucked-up Cro-Magnon hog. To this day, for obvious reasons, that totally humiliating incident, endless source of humor though it is, tops my list of Life's Shittiest Moments. Although I've come to realize that it aptly epitomized my comedy career in Boston: *Sucked.*

David Cross

I'm no pilot.
Never logged a second of flight time in my life.

But I did fly a plane in *It's a Mad Mad Mad Mad World*. And on the big screen, I looked like I really knew what the hell I was doing.

A few years after the movie came out, I hopped a small plane, a Twin Beech Bonanza, from Grand Junction, Colorado, to nearby Aspen. And when I say small, I mean tiny. This thing sold all eight of its seats, including the copilot's. That's where I sat, right next to the captain.

So both of us introduced ourselves, and as I was getting situated, he asked me, "How would you like to help me run the check?"

"The check?" I said. "But I don't know how."

I must have insulted him or something, because from that point on, he didn't speak another word to me. Didn't even look my way. And it sure wasn't because he had to concentrate hard. I mean, it was a bright, sunny day, and the visibility was spectacular. So why was he snubbing me like this?

When we landed, I thanked him for a smooth flight, but he continued to ignore me. Turned his back, even! What the fuck was his problem? A few minutes later, I went to get my bag and ran into one of the flight attendants. "Was the pilot mad at me?" I asked her.

"Yeah," she told me. "He asked you to run the check, and if you didn't want to, you could have just said you didn't feel like it. You didn't have to tell him you don't know how."

Apparently, this guy had seen me in *It's a Mad Mad Mad Mad World* and thought I could actually fly! He just figured I was lying to him, being a stuck-up movie star. Holy Christ! I thought. We trusted him with our lives and he couldn't even separate fact from fiction! Who knew how many others had been brainwashed by my brilliant performance?

It was then I vowed never to play a superhero.

Buddy Hackett

During the run

of my second series, *Caesar's Hour,* I became

concerned that a particular comedy sketch wasn't up to snuff. So I summoned my gaggle of crack writers, which included Meathead Sr., Carl Reiner, to an emergency dinner powwow. For some reason, the guys showed up at the restaurant expecting me to issue some lucid comedic directives. But instead, they encountered After-Hours Sid, who'd obviously been grabbin' the grape and was a bit off-kilter. Okay, bombed, blotto, tanked. Get the picture?

As I was attempting to order broiled filet of sole, I suddenly lost consciousness and my head plopped into a nearby bowl of coleslaw. Knowing they'd have to quickly devise a plan to keep this incident out of the tabloids, the troops, marshaled by Reiner, did as any good comedy scribes would do with such a predicament: they worked it into a sketch.

"So, Inspector," began one writer, standing over my comatose corpse with a steak knife, "this is undoubtedly the murder weapon, which makes the waiter a chief suspect!" Passersby, many of whom normally would have approached to pay their respects to Caesar, declined, seeing as an important rehearsal was obviously going on here. But one group of diners, oblivious to the fact that this was a *closed* rehearsal, sidled up to say hello. Panicked, Reiner blurted, "Let us pray," and he and his colleagues abruptly bowed their heads in feigned supplication, effectively camouflaging their boozy boss, who, as it so happened, was already deep in prayer. And coleslaw.

For nearly an hour, the boys, laboring heroically to defend my honor, came up with some of their best material ever—or so I was later told. When I finally surfaced from my swamp of slaw, groggy and soggy, I picked up right where I'd left off. "And a side of shoestring potatoes with that sole," I ordered from no waiter in particular. My Round Table of knights just stared at me. "What?" I said, self-conscious at last. "Something's in my teeth?"

Sid Caesar

For some people,
attending the theater is akin to BarcaLounging

in the privacy of their own home—it's a chance to get some R&R. Sometimes, patrons will even doze off during a performance. (That always bolsters an actor's spirits.) And then you have those who are simply oblivious to the fact that *other beings* are in the room.

When I was on Broadway doing *A Funny Thing Happened on the Way to the Forum*, we were midway through a scene in the first act when a mammoth man, seated toward the middle of the second row, decided it was time for a potty break. I mean, this guy was so huge, he had his own climate. Therefore, when he stood up, fourteen others were forced to do likewise so he could pass. And to make matters worse, he moved at the speed of sludge.

It was inevitable, then, that this human tidal wave, this mass of molten lava, would draw considerable attention to himself. Even the actors broke form and watched as he *s-l-o-w-l-y* rose and *s-l-o-w-l-y* made his way down the row and out the exit. It must have taken a good five minutes. And the funniest thing was, he seemed utterly unaware of the distraction he was creating. It was as though

he'd been watching the World Series and this was the seventh-inning stretch—*Miller Time.* I half expected him to return with a six-pack and a brat.

When the audience, which had gone from mild tittering to wild guffawing, calmed down, I blithely exclaimed, "So, where was I?" and resumed the scene. The show, as you know, must go on. And so it did. Until, at the end of Act One, Lava Boy made his grand reentry. As before, he *s-l-o-w-l-y* made his way toward the second row, and *s-l-o-w-l-y* squeezed past the same fourteen patrons who'd once again risen so as to avoid being crushed by his girth.

Coincidentally, my last line as the curtain fell on the first act was "Fine, just fine!" So, upon exclaiming it once to my fellow actors, I began screaming it repeatedly at Andre the Giant, who remained thoroughly inattentive to my redirected exasperation. In fact, it wasn't until the final curtain call, when, after taking our bows, I and the entire cast dramatically acknowledged him, that he finally realized something was afoot. Although he still looked puzzled, as if to say, "Did I miss something while I was *ON THE CAN*?!"

I'm just guessing here, but somehow I don't think drama scholars had this scenario in mind when they coined the term *Theater of the Absurd*.

Nathan Lane

One of my

best friends has this annoying habit of grabbing food
off my plate.

One night, we went out for Japanese, and after the main course, he excused himself
to go to the men's room. When I asked if he wanted me to order him dessert while
he was gone, he declined. But I knew him too well. He'd refuse his portion and
eat half of mine.

When dessert arrived, he was still in the men's room. So I took the liberty of
mixing my leftover wasabi, a bright greenish spice, with my green tea ice cream,
knowing full well he'd devour the whole damned bowl. Seconds later, just as
I'd predicted, he returned and went straight for my plate.

At first, it seemed as though he was really enjoying it. But after only a few bites, he froze. His brow furrowed, his eyes welled up with tears, and he began panting like a pooch. As I watched him squirm, the Franz in me thought, *What's da matta? Too spicy for da little girlie man? Look at da wussy girlie man bawling like a little baby. I could easily crush his little baby head with my pectorals*. In layman's terms, I finally had the upper hand.

Unfortunately, my sadistic little lesson had no long-term effect. Days later, he was chowing my chow as always. Some folks just never learn.

Kevin Nealon

The audience

of my show, *Sabrina, The Teenage Witch*, is, aptly enough, mostly kids.

So I'm never shocked when full-grown people don't know me from the meter maid.

A while ago, while on tour in Denver, I was driven around town by a very courteous man who, upon delivering me to my hotel after a gig, said, "Caroline, while you're in Denver, if you need a lift anywhere, please don't hesitate to call." He then handed me a card, which he asked me to sign. Now, keep in mind that it was late at night, I was extremely tired, and I'd just signed post-show autographs for a thousand fans. So when I took his card I reflexively scrawled, "*BEST WITCHES* (in very large, obnoxious letters), *Caroline Rhea—Aunt Hilda*."

Just as I was inking the final dramatic swoop, though, the driver, who'd been drumming his fingers on the roof (apparently I was taking longer than expected), began to make small talk. "So, Caroline," he asked, "what do you do for a living?" My hand came to an abrupt halt. Huh? He didn't know about the magic spells and the talking cat and the . . .

Then I noticed the small print below where I'd signed: *Passenger Signature*. All this guy wanted was a receipt, and here I was playing Norma Desmond. I wanted to disappear. I tried to disappear. After all, that's what my character, Aunt Hilda, would have done. But, alas, I'm no witch. I just play one on TV.

Caroline Rhea

As a lifelong

Asian American, I can state with a fair amount of certainty that the beloved Raggedy Ann doll is not Chinese.

In other words, she looks nothing like Connie Chung. Or me, either, for that matter.

Which is why, for whatever reason, I once played her at FAO Schwarz. Raggedy Ann, not Connie Chung. And, man, was I good. That doll and I were as one. For a while there, I actually became a boneless, brainless hunk of synthetic mush. And that's no easy feat.

So there I was, flouncing around the store like a coked-up Muppet, when I noticed that some of the shoppers, mainly kids, looked puzzled. Right away, I sensed the problem. No matter how much makeup I applied, no matter how doll-like I acted, I couldn't disguise my Asian heritage, especially the eyes.

For the most part, though, people were polite and let me do my shtick. But one little boy, whose parents obviously forgot to school him in the art of tact, apparently decided I was desecrating this classic American plaything. Before I knew what was happening, he charged toward me, booted me in the shins, and cried "You're not Raggedy Ann! She has *round* eyes!"

Busted. The little punk had blown my cover! Now all his fellow tots were wise to my charade. Would they attack me, too? I hoped not. Though as I stood there, nursing my wound, I imagined the next day's headlines: RAGGEDY ANN IMPOSTOR LYNCHED BY PINT-SIZED MOB. And to think, I almost took the Barbie gig.

Margaret Cho

During my time

at *Saturday Night Live*, Billy Crystal and I performed a somewhat bizarre sketch

in which I played a guy named Brad Allen, a stereotypical overprotective corporate father. The premise of the sketch was this: Brad would hypnotize his teenage daughter's prospective suitors by having them stare into the flames of his fireplace. Once under his spell, the young men were queried about their true intentions.

Fresh from doing one of his Joe Franklin sketches, for which he had donned a bald pate, Billy, who played the daughter's punk date, had had little time to change costumes, and so wore a hippie-style wig over the pate. Upon hypnotizing him, I asked, "So, what are you going to do with my daughter?" "Take her to the movies," Billy replied. "And then?" "And then I'm gonna buy her a hamburger." "And then?" "And then I'm gonna have sex with her."

Wrong answer. And wrong answers, per script instruction, required that I smack Billy on the noggin. Which I playfully did,

five times in all. With each blow I delivered, though, the wig slipped farther down the back of his head, gradually revealing the Uncle Fester–like cranium beneath. Of course, the audience, upon noticing this, went nuts.

Initially, Billy and I were staring so intently into the fire that neither of us noticed. We just figured our comedic interplay was absolutely hysterical. Toward the end of the scene, however, when Julia Louis-Dreyfus, who played the daughter, descended the stairs to meet her date, she took one look at Billy's askew do and lost it. By then, the audience, too, was nearly dead from laughter, although not, we finally realized, as a result of our rapier wits and brilliant acting. Touted as two of the show's supposedly brightest talents, Billy and I had been upstaged by a lopsided hairpiece, which I proceeded to readjust, which got even more laughs, cheap laughs, which, I suppose, were better than none at all.

Martin Short

I know this

great little deli in the St. Louis airport.

I know it only because I was once delayed in St. Louis on my way back to L.A. Why the hell else would I go to a deli in the St. Louis airport?

Our plane had mechanical problems—the air-conditioning was on the blink—so they kept us waiting in the terminal while the mechanics tinkered. It was early evening, and I hadn't eaten lunch, so I was starving here; that thumb-sized bag of airline peanuts hadn't even dented my appetite. And to make matters worse, I'd been told this wouldn't be a dinner flight. So one of the airline employees suggested I grab a sandwich at the deli down the hall. Which I did, posthaste. But when I brought this gorgeous, mouth-watering creation back to the waiting area, no one was there. Apparently, the plane had been fixed, reboarded, and was ready to roll. I was the last man standing.

But I had this sandwich! This big, beautiful sandwich! Though it would be rude, I knew, to chow in front of my fellow peanut-eating passengers. So I took a quick, luscious bite and left my baby on a nearby ashtray. I almost cried.

Once on the plane, I was, fortunately, seated in the first row. I say fortunately, because fifteen minutes later, the plane hadn't moved an inch; the air-conditioning was still busted. Everyone, they announced, would have to deplane. Again. Well, the second I heard that, I was up and out, bounding frantically down the jetway, hoping against all hope that my sandwich hadn't been swiped.

To my surprise, it was sitting on the ashtray just as I'd left it. Come to papa, I thought, ready to devour it whole. Then, behind me, I heard a little girl's voice exclaim, "Mommy! That man took a dirty old sandwich off that ashtray!" What did she know? She was just a kid. Indignant, I made a big show of savoring every morsel. "Mmmmmmm, delicious!"

"Eeeeyooo!" the little girl cried. "Now he's *eating* it!"

I even heard a guy behind me at the ticket counter say, "See that guy with the glasses? He's the one with the sandwich."

Already, I was a legend in St. Louis. And not in a good way. But I was too busy stuffing my face to care.

Stan Freberg

In some ways,

my wife, Mary, and I are vastly different.

She's a farmer's daughter with an advanced degree in history, and I'm the stock of artists. Thus, whereas I'm often dramatic, she has absolutely no sense of performance. Whereas I'm fond of occasional euphemism (okay, white lies), she's straightforward and honest to a fault. Once in a while, though, she'll humor my devious bent.

Shortly after the birth of our first child, Phoebe, I brought the family into New York City for a tour of the Metropolitan Museum of Art, a favorite haunt of mine. With our child secured to my bosom in one of those yuppie papooses, I readied myself for a day of cultural enrichment. But even before we began, I realized my back wasn't going to withstand this getup for long. Glancing around, I noticed a stash of wheelchairs in one corner. That gave me an idea. Now if only I could get my wife to play along.

I must have been convincing, because moments later I was wheeling Mary and child amid the Rembrandts. "You look too healthy," I subtly reminded her. "Remember, you're convalescing." But as the hours passed, she grew increasingly uneasy.

Everyone was convinced she was handicapped, even the maître d' at lunch, who, after we finished, commanded his waiters to help this poor woman back to her wheelchair.

That was more than she could bear. Angry and thoroughly humiliated, she refused to continue with my sick little charade and demanded we leave the museum at once. But she'd killed, I insisted. They loved her. Mary just glared at me. It seemed no amount of praise could allay her misgivings.

Still, as we exited the building and went our separate ways, my wife, despite her fierce protests, remained dedicated to the role in which I'd cast her. Not out of loyalty to me or any thespian code, mind you, but because she was terrified her lie would be discovered. Regardless of motive, I was touched. With tears in my eyes, I watched as masterfully, heart-wrenchingly, she limped three blocks up Fifth Avenue to the nearest bus stop. Notify the Academy, I thought. A star is born.

John Lithgow

My dad

is a strange bird and a constant source of amusement.

Even though he's seventy now and has two artificial hips, in his mind he's still the spry vaudevillian/gymnast he once was. To prove this to himself and to the world, every day, at Miami's South Beach, near where he lives, he hurls himself off a pier and into the ocean. Forty feet below.

And it's not just his outward behavior that's off-kilter. For instance, in his wallet, in those brittle plastic photo holders that most people throw out, he keeps various snapshots that are, for one reason or another, near and dear to him. One is a lovely shot of his boat at sunset. Another is of four leotard-clad gymnasts doing splits above his head. Still another is of our dog, Archie. Archie is dead. And the most prized one of all is of my dad himself, twenty and muscle-bound, posing in a swimsuit on some beach in Chicago. It must be hilarious when he swaps these with strangers. Stranger: "This is my oldest son, Joey. He's ten." Dad: "This is my favorite pet, Archie. He's dead."

But Dad's active and healthy and that's what matters most. In fact, he still coaches gymnastics, as he has since I was little (which explains the gymnasts-in-leotards picture in his wallet). Every day, from age five till I turned eighteen, he dragged me to the gym and made me schlep equipment. And every day he made me work out for hours on end as if I were training for the Olympics. And every day he reminded me that I wasn't "genetically made to be a gymnast." So basically, I busted my hump and developed eating disorders for the fun of it.

I didn't truly appreciate the grueling torture he put me through until 1983, when I got my big break on *The Tonight Show*. Oddly enough, my gymnastic ability turned out to be my ticket to stardom. My act: reciting poetry while doing a handstand. If it weren't for Dad, I never would have been able to do a handstand in the first place. Needless to say, he was really proud of me. Still is. Although why the dead family pet gets more space in his wallet than I do, I'll never know. On second thought, maybe it's better that way.

Victoria Jackson

Show business

is a breeding ground for heartache,
 failed marriages, and drug addiction.

Those problems aside, I also suffer from an obsessive need to
know everyone's net worth. You might say I'm a net-worth
junkie. Chalk it up to intense curiosity, but nearly every time I
meet someone, I just have to probe their financial situation. And
the more they're worth, the more depressed I get. Admittedly,
it's a strange compulsion, but it's not as though I'm licking
elevator buttons.

Of course, anyone who knows me well is used to my monetary
queries. Tim Conway, in particular, who's been a pal of mine
for years, is well aware of my disorder. A while ago, both of us
attended a party with a well-known horse trainer named Gary
Jones. Jones, who lives quite well, has a thriving business.
I just couldn't help myself. "So, Gary," I asked, "what's a guy
like you worth?"

"See for yourself," he replied, handing me a hefty folder
containing his official financial statement—complete with gains,
losses, and net worth to the penny!

My knees buckled. This couldn't be happening. Usually it
took some cajoling. Soon, though, I realized I'd been duped.
Conway had set me up. He's a wily one, that Conway.
Wonder what he's worth.

Harvey Korman

Some years ago,
a good friend of mine,

comedian Dave Thomas, was offered a six-week trial television series, *The Dave Thomas Comedy Show,* the premiere of which featured Dave, myself, and Martin Short doing a sketch about the fear of flying. We even wore ridiculous toupees that stood on end to illustrate just how freaked out we really were. It was a great bit of physical comedy.

Well, the timing couldn't have been worse. The big night arrived and Dave's house was packed with friends and family, all of whom beamed with pride. Look, some murmured, there's our Dave. On television! But only moments after his show began, a news bulletin crept slowly across the screen. Something about a small plane that had gone down in a nearby town. An unfortunate scenario, for sure, but a relatively minor annoyance as far as the show was concerned. On-screen, Dave's monologue continued unabated.

Though not for long. Abruptly, he was preempted by live shots of the gruesome wreckage. Survivors stumbling about. Fire-fighters staving off the blaze. What a mess. It couldn't get much worse than this, I thought. Then the station cut back to the three of us in our goofy wigs joking about airplane disasters. Okay, so I was wrong.

Miraculously, as we learned later that night, the victims of the horrific crash had survived. Most of them, anyway. Dave's series was canceled shortly thereafter.

Chevy Chase

In the days

before I began pummeling some of the world's best-loved pop tunes,

I was a phone freak extraordinaire. My friend and I would squander inordinate amounts of time devising ways to harass people. And it wasn't the usual stuff. Seymour Butts, we figured, deserved a break already.

One afternoon, we discovered, quite accidentally, that rubbing a screwdriver against the bare wires of a disassembled mouthpiece produced an ear-piercing static sound. Pure gold. Like finding the key to the old man's liquor cabinet, only better. We couldn't wait to put it to good use. Good, of course, is a relative term.

So we randomly chose a name from the phone book—a Mrs. Johnson—and rang her up.

"Hello," answered a feeble voice. This woman was obviously ancient.

"Ma'am, this is George Bernay with Pacific Bell," I told her in my newly basso profundo timbre. "I'm calling to let you know we're fusing together all the trunk lines in your area."

"I like birds."

"Um, maybe you don't understand, Mrs. Johnson," I continued. "Our men are working with very high-voltage equipment, so please *don't* pick up your phone for the next half hour. If you do, it will send a massive surge of current through the lines. And that would be *extremely dangerous*."

"Okay," she replied, a bit more lucidly than before.

Ten minutes later, we called her again. The phone rang about a hundred times before she finally picked up. "Hello?" she answered, tentatively.

"*Scrrrrreeeeeeech!*" went screwdriver against wire, mimicking the sound of coursing electricity.

With a horrified gasp, she hung up.

But we were relentless. Immediately I redialed. "Mrs. Johnson, what have you done?!" Then, as though I were barking into a walkie-talkie, "Lineman number seven is down! Repeat: Lineman number seven is down!"

On the other end, silence. Then, dial tone. Next victim!

Weird Al Yankovic

One thing's for sure:

American males like their meat. My father was no exception.

Greens never touched his plate or, therefore, his intestines. "Salad is for cows," he'd say. Consequently, owing to their infrequency and intensity, his bowel movements were major events in the Klein household, a simple but nice Bronx apartment with three and a half rooms. And one toilet.

One morning at breakfast, my father, who'd not had a satisfying b.m. in some time, got The Look. We all knew The Look, feared The Look. "That's it!" he blurted suddenly and bounded into the bathroom. It was, we all agreed, a close call. But only seconds later, he yelled for me to bring him, of all things, an umbrella. An *umbrella*? Not to mention the fact that he expected me to approach the throne while he was doing the king's business. But, loyal son that I was, I didn't question the odd request. I just did my duty so he could do his.

Slowly, cautiously, I opened the bathroom door, unsure of what I'd find on the other side. As it turned out, my mother's undergarments, all sopping wet, were hanging on a clothesline above the toilet. It was like a rain forest in there, and my father, perched on the can in coat and tie, was getting doused. I handed him the umbrella, which he quickly opened and held aloft to stave off the elements. He was no Gene Kelly, that's for sure. But even in his misery, he recognized the humor of his absurd predicament. We both exploded with laughter.

Then it thundered.

I ran for cover.

The storm, I knew, was upon us.

Robert Klein

Ronald Reagan

is a favorite impression
of mine.

It must be a favorite of his, too, because the ex-president and I have become quite close over the years. I even attended his first inauguration, in 1980. It certainly was a grand affair, but mostly I remember how fun it was. And not just the dancing.

After the swearing-in ceremony, I was relaxing with some friends in Patricia Neal's suite at the Watergate Hotel. We were in party limbo here, stopped over on the way to the big bash at the White House. So a friend of mine suggested I use my talent for evil and phone Bette Davis in the voice of Jimmy Stewart. Happy for the chance to flex my chops, I obliged.

Amazingly (well, not *that* amazingly), Bette really believed I was Jimmy. Apparently, the two were rather close chums. But then she started asking me personal questions, questions that only the real Jimmy Stewart could answer. "Bette," I finally had to fess up, "It's Rich Little."

Well, this just infuriated her, and she demanded to speak with the person who'd put me up to this nonsense. "I'll never have anything to do with you or Rich Little again!" she screamed at my friend, then hung up.

When I ran into Jimmy and the president at the inaugural ball that evening, I told them what had happened. Both thought it was hilarious, Jimmy especially. Bette, I explained, was furious and had vowed never to speak to me again. At this, Reagan seemed puzzled. "Bette's a tough old bird, but she's got a great sense of humor," he said. "Let me try to straighten things out."

So we stole out of the party and went to use the phone in the offices off the Lincoln bedroom. Bette's number was dialed, and when she answered, Reagan took the receiver. "Hello, Bette, this is Ronald Reagan."

After a long pause, Reagan put down the phone. He seemed stunned.

"What did she say?" we asked.

"Well," deadpanned the newly minted leader of the Free World, "she said, 'Fuck you, Rich Little!' and hung up."

For the second time that day, he'd been sworn into office.

Rich Little

Not to sound

pompous, but people recognize me all the time.

"Hey, look," they'll say, "it's Carol Burnett!" Or they'll really mangle things and ask, "Aren't you Carol Lawrence?" Carol, Carol, Carol. I feel like Jan Brady. It's dogged me nearly my entire career.

Back when I was a guest on the game show *Password,* audience members were invited to question the celebrity panelists during commercial breaks. "Carol," one lady asked me, "what was it like being married to Robert Goulet?" Then she sat down and patiently waited for an answer. But even though it was the real Carol who was married to Bob Goulet, instead of correcting her, I played along. Sure, it was yet another slap in the face, but it was just too good an opportunity to pass up.

"Well," I replied, "he's a total son of a bitch and I divorced his ass!"

The woman was speechless. Not the answer she'd expected. The crew, however, was splitting seams. I think Allen Ludden, the host, nearly peed his pants. After the show, however, I became somewhat concerned that my offhanded comment, though harmless in intention, would upset Carol.

Sure enough, a few months later, she spotted me at some crowded Hollywood function and immediately cut a swath in my direction. Oh, crap. I was gonna get reamed, I knew it. So I cowered and braced myself for the onslaught. Soon we were standing face to face. "I heard about *Password*," she informed me, smiling radiantly. Wait. Smiling radiantly? That could mean only one thing: she was angrier than I thought.

"Carol," I blurted, "I can expl—"

"Not necessary," she interjected. "You took the words right out of my mouth."

I was relieved, not to mention highly amused. Fortunately, she had a sense of humor. In this business, you can't take yourself too seriously. When she left a stranger approached and asked for my autograph. "Ms. Burnett," he said, "I'm a really big fan."

Vicki Lawrence

Back when

he was just a pup, Woody Allen
would often watch me perform

at the Blue Angel in New York City. To this day, he maintains that
my conversational manner influenced his own comedy stylings.
In fact, he says I impacted not only his career, but his life. That's
hefty praise coming from anyone, not to mention one of
the greatest comedic wits of our time.

For years, I continued to receive Woody's compliments, but only
secondhand through the showbiz grapevine. Never once did
I hear them straight from the man himself. Then one afternoon
Woody and I both happened to show up at the same time for lunch
at the Russian Tea Room in midtown Manhattan. I was already
seated, and when I saw him walk in I flagged down the maître d'
and dispatched him with the summons, "Tell Mr. Allen the
man who changed his life would like to see him."

Upon receiving my vicarious invitation, Woody immediately
shuffled over to my table, smiled, and warmly embraced me.
Then he said, by way of reply, "Actually, Mort, it hasn't been
that great. Can you change it back?"

Ingrate.

Mort Sahl

I'm not a comic

who uses foul language for shock value,

but I will use it if it serves the story. In this particular case, it *is* the story.

Inevitably, a toddler is going to hear, and then repeat, a profanity. Just accept it. Unless your son's name is Opie, at some point in toddlerhood you're going to hear a gleeful, high-pitched curse.

Now parents, listen closely. Your first instinct might be to laugh, or perhaps scold.

No.

The only correct response is to *ignore*.

Absolutely, positively ignore. Don't bring any attention to it whatsoever. And by all means, don't do what I did: videotape it.

Learn from me.

The first time one of my two-year-olds repeated a curse, I'll admit, it was funny, and I laughed.

Little did I know I had created a monster.

Listen, when a two-year-old sees that he can get a reaction from Mommy and Daddy, his thought pattern is this:

I'll do it again.

And he did it quite often.

It never really posed much of a problem, because we were the only ones who he would say it to.

Then one day my eighty-seven-year-old grandmother was over at the house.

An eighty-seven-year-old playfully jostling a two-year-old and then . . .

"Nonna, you fuck."

My wife and I froze, hoping it didn't register.

"Nonna, you fuck."

That one was loud and clear. What followed was a "Nonna, you fuck" medley. All types of deliveries. Singsong, rapid-fire, couple of hold-the-last-noters, and my personal favorite, the gravelly voiced one with a scream chaser.

He just kept at it as Nonna watched and watched.

Now, as far as what happened afterward, I'm almost afraid to tell you. I don't want future parents to take the consequences of a cursing baby lightly. This story should serve as a warning to them and not as something amusing. But I'm not going to hold back the truth. Here's what happened.

As the barrage of "Nonna, you fucks" continued, Grandma turned to me and with a puzzled look said: "I think he wants fudge."

We didn't deserve to be that lucky. She had no idea what he was saying. The more he said it, the hungrier she thought he was. She gave him some fudge and was never the wiser.

No one was hurt, no one was offended, and we let out a huge sigh of relief.

Of course, soon after that we realized that our two-year-old had a whole new thought pattern.

Say *fuck*, get fudge.

Ray Romano

It's the bane

of my existence that I'm a woman.

God, I would be such a great man! And I'd have only the finest, USDA-choice ladies. See, I know how to treat women. They're suckers for old-fashioned stuff and dumb little gestures. And here's another hint: actually *remembering* shit is huge. Like, the shirt she wore on the first date. Or, if that sort of stuff's too taxing, her *birthday*! And this whole business about going Dutch, and not opening doors—*ridiculous*! Oh, no, no, no. In my world, the guy pays, the guy opens the door. Don't give me this "I thought you were a liberated woman" bullshit. I guess what I'm saying here is, guys are fools. And believe me, I've dated enough losers to know just how true that is.

Though, I admit, I'm at least partially to blame for my misfortune. You see, I tend to date inappropriately young men. The guys, of course, never think it's a problem. It's always me who has to explain, "Don't you get it? I'm your Mrs. Robinson." But invariably they'll reply, "Who?" Or, "Wow, she sounds like a nice lady." Kids. One time I dated a guy who told me, "Don't worry, I once dated a lady who was *thirty-five*." "First off," I informed him, "the fact that you referred to her as a *lady* is a *big problem*. Secondly, for God's sake, man! I'm old enough to be your *older sister*!"

Basically, most of my young stud muffins just want to party all night, every night, or sit around and play Nintendo, or move into my house and have me support them. And they're always flummoxed that I can't stay out late on weeknights. It's like, *working woman here*! Got a job. Know what that is? Some of them probably can't even spell job, much less hold one. I once had to show a guy how to open a checking account. Never had one in his life. Shortly after that, he brought me his first utility bill—literally dropped it out of his mouth onto the coffee table like a dog would a freshly killed bird. "Okay," he said, ears cocked, "what happens next?" Jesus, where do I dig 'em up?

When it comes down to it, I'm just an old cowpoke. I can't keep up with the kids like I used to. What I need is a real man, a man like Steve the bald security guard on *The Jerry Springer Show*. What a hunky specimen he is. We talkin' future husband material here. But aside from his brawny masculinity, I dig him because he's a Chicago homeboy, just as I'm a Chicago homegirl. He even asked me out once, after we'd appeared together on the *Billboard* Music Awards, during which I'd plopped myself on his lap and proclaimed my

affections for him before millions of viewers. After the show he was, like, in full Chicago accent, which I adore, "Kath, ya know, I'd like ta take ya out to a nice dinner sometime when yer in Chicaago. I won't ax fer yer number. I'll jis' give ya mine. An' I live right by da studio if ya wanna come and hang out er whaadever. I dunno."

Now that's a man's man. I mean it. What a catch, and sweet guy, too. If everything works out, I plan to be on *Suddenly Susan* for one more year, move back to Chicago, buy a Frank Lloyd Wright home, and live there with my new husband Steve. Of course, he doesn't know those exact particulars yet. But he should know this: I AM GOING TO *PUT OUT*!

Kathy Griffin

Few people

know I was once a burlesque stripper.

(Hey, we all had to start somewhere, right?) But feather boas and slinky lingerie weren't my style.

The high point (or low point, as it were) of my act came when the stage manager, in sync with the closing punch line, ripped off my trousers, leaving me standing center stage in nothing but my trademark red bloomers. That is, when I remembered to *wear* my trademark red bloomers.

One evening, during a run at Broadway's Gaiety Theater, I was late for work and just plain forgot to don my crimson underduds. But no one knew that, least of all the stage manager. So toward the end of the performance, right on cue, he tore off my pants as he had a hundred nights before. Immediately, a collective gasp arose from the audience, followed by wild guffawing. It seems that Red Jr. was flapping in the breeze.

But I couldn't have been more oblivious. They were laughing, fer Chrissake! Hey, I've arrived! I must be hilarious! I thought, lapping up the praise.

Then I glanced down. That night, the only things red on Red were my cheeks. And not just the ones on my face. I was mortified, but I laughed louder than anyone. Of course, it was at that point I realized I wasn't big in the business.

Red Buttons

The mere thought
of it brings a smile to my face.

Because it was funny, sure, but also because it was incredibly erotic. Mmmm, I get aroused just thinking about it. What a sexy, sexy time that was. It was my Awakening, if you will, the point in my career at which I realized, Hey, guy, it doesn't get any better than this.

My comedy cohort, David Cross, and I were invited to appear on HBO's annual *Comic Relief* benefit. Being fairly new on the block, we were honored to be included in such a widely acclaimed program. After noodling for a while, we finally decided to reenact a sketch we'd done only a couple of times in small clubs. Its premise was this: I played a highly gullible guy whose friend, played by David, ultimately dupes him into getting completely naked in a public place. In this case, the place was Radio City Music Hall before an audience of thousands. I suppose the stunt worked mostly because I'm not that well known. Marlon Brando, for example, never could (nor should) have pulled it off.

After streaking through the auditorium, I ran up onstage and stood there next to David, completely nude, cupping my privates with both hands. Staring out at the ocean of people, I suddenly felt this surge shoot through my genitals. In a matter of moments, I became so engorged that had I been even slightly more well-endowed, mere hands might not have sufficiently cloaked my mass of throbbing manhood. It was embarrassing, sure, but I couldn't help it. In fact, I began to enjoy it. The audience was so incredibly hot. It was flirting with me, teasing me. The winks, the feather boas—Jesus, it wanted me! And you should have seen the ass on that room. It was sexing me up.

Only after my piece—pardon the lingo— was done did I feel nervous and a bit ashamed. Perhaps because I'd grown flaccid and blood was once again feeding my brain, which reminded me that the act was through and I was just plain old Bob now. While it lasted, though, my naked stint in one of our country's most hallowed halls was the attainment of every actor's dream. Also, having never been a porn star, it was the best onstage foreplay I've ever experienced.

Bob Odenkirk

One afternoon,

in my hometown of Santa Barbara, I was browsing

in my favorite antique shop when I noticed that a middle-aged couple was trailing me. And not very deftly, I might add. They were whispering loudly. And pointing.

So, when I thought they weren't looking, I made a quick exit. But these people were tenacious, especially the woman, who caught up with me on the street, excited that she'd finally spied a bona fide star. Or so she thought.

"You're that guy, that, that comedian," she stammered, floundering for a name.

"No, madam," I interrupted. "You must be mistaken. My name is Edlinger, Dr. Steven Edlinger, noted gynecologist and pediatric taxidermist."

"But you're a spitting image of Jonathan Winters," she finally recalled, oblivious to my outrageous credentials. "My husband and I are from the Midwest, and you're the first star we've ever seen. We'd really love to get your autograph."

She seemed sweet enough, but I was having too much fun. "Listen, lady," I told her, "I've been mistaken for that idiot Winters one too many times! Here's my card. Do you have any children? Or small animals?"

"I'm so sorry," she finally conceded, still unfazed. "I guess I was wrong. Howard, you *asshole*!" she shrieked to her husband, who waited in the car, "I *told* you it wasn't him!"

Jonathan Winters

So I'm in Miami

for the Supa Bowl, when who do I run into

at one of the pregame shindigs but k.d. lang. Ya know, the singa with the "constant craving." Anyhow, so we start yappin', and she says to me, she says, "Which team are you rooting for?" "The Broncos," I tell huh. And she goes, "But how come your're not rooting for the underdog?" "Now wait a minute," I says, "I could go both ways." "Fran," she cracks, "that's just what I'm afraid of!" Oy, did I blush. That *was* a compliment, right?"

76

Fran Drescher

When I was single,
Frank Sinatra helped me out with
a lot of girls.

I remember one night, I was sitting with this gorgeous broad in the lounge at the Sands Hotel in Vegas. I knew she was somebody I could score with if things went right. So I went up to Frank, who was at a nearby table, and said, "Listen, Frank, I'm with this girl, and if you came over and said hello to us, it would help me a lot."

"No problem," he told me.

So after a while, just like he said, he walked over to my table and went, "Hey, Don, it's nice to see you and the beautiful lady . . ."

I looked up and said, very loud, "Frank, *not now*! Can't you see I'm *with somebody*! For God's sake! How do *I* know if your album's going to sell? Just get out of my life!"

He laughed his ass off.

Then he had seven guys pick me up and throw me out of the casino.

Don Rickles

I was eight years old
the first time I *really* laughed at something.

I was watching Sid Caesar's *Caesar's Hour* on television, and they were doing
a takeoff on *The King and I*. Sid Caesar came out—bald head, short pants, bare
feet—struck the Yul Brynner pose, grabbed his foot, and screamed, "Ow, who's
been smokin' in the palace!?" For some reason, it made me laugh and laugh.
I knew then that comedy was what I wanted to do.

Billy Crystal

Some years ago,
while on tour in New Zealand,

I had the opportunity to observe a fascinating ritual. It all began pleasantly enough. My wife and I were treated to a lavish dinner at a fashionable Auckland eatery. All in all, it was a pretty swanky evening. Mostly.

After we'd gorged ourselves and the dishes had been cleared, we sat around talking and drinking. Then—and here's where it gets good—our waiter approached and placed a small cup of toothpicks on the table. Moments later, the cup was raised by one gentleman, who took a pick, then passed the chalice to his neighbor—like this thing was the Holy Grail or something! When our turn came, my wife and I politely declined. But we were the only ones to pass. I noticed that everyone else sported wood.

Now New Zealand's finest were poised to (banjo music, please)
Let the Picking Begin. As they did so, in unison, they looked like players in some freaky backwoods orchestra—*Deliverance* meets the Boston Pops.

My wife subtly averted her eyes, thoroughly appalled. I, on the other hand, stared on, completely transfixed. Hell, I figured, every culture has its postmeal traditions. Besides, this paled in comparison with, say, ancient Roman–style mass vomiting. See, everything's relative.

82

Shelley Berman

The Diller home

has been party central plenty of times.

But the most memorable bash occurred just a few years ago, at Halloween. The place was really decked out with all kinds of gadgets and gizmos and Halloweeny decor. My favorite touch, however, were these so-called rug screamers, which, when placed under a rug and stepped upon, emitted bloodcurdling, crap-in-your-pants shrieks.

Among the invited revelers at this ghoulfest was my eighty-something beau, who'd been out of town and was supposed to meet me at the house a few hours before the party began. As it happened, on his way from the airport, he absentmindedly ran a red light and plowed right into the side of a brand-new Mercedes. There was carnage galore, or so I was told. His Cadillac and the Mercedes were reduced to twisted hunks of steel. Fortunately, my hunk and the guy he hit were unhurt. I get emotional just thinking about it. I mean, they were *really* nice cars.

By the time the tow truck dropped him at the house, my man was, of course, a frazzled, nervous wreck. (Having your life flash before your eyes will do that to you.) But it wasn't his day. Just as his heart was finally beginning to regulate, he opened the front door, carefully shut off the alarm, and walked right onto the screaming rug. God did he freak out when the thing began howling bloody murder! In fact, he became so mortified that he called in the SWAT team to investigate. Imagine their amusement when the boys in blue discovered that their culprit required four double-A batteries. I'm sure they're still laughing. I know I am.

Phyllis Diller

I don't laugh

very easily, but when I find something funny

the whole room knows it. Back when I was writing for Sid Caesar's *Your Show of Shows*, the gang of us went out one night to see the Italian comedy *Big Deal on Madonna Street*, a gangster spoof starring Marcello Mastroianni. The plot revolves around this clownish band of pseudowiseguy jewel thieves who scheme to rip off the local jewelry store. In order to accomplish this, they move into the apartment next door so as to gain entry through the wall that separates the two. But these guys were the most inept clods I'd ever seen. In the end, after hours of toil, they finally break through the wall, on the other side of which is not the jewelry store, but their own kitchen.

Although I haven't watched the film in some time, I remember that night very clearly. Most of all, aside from the masterful comedic interplay, I remember an incessant, high-pitched feminine laugh coming from somewhere in the audience. It took a while for me to realize that it was coming from me. I'd never seen anything so hilarious in my life. In fact, it even spawned a sketch, which was hilarious in its own right.

Instead of pirating a jewelry store, our gang of misfit burglars plotted to pilfer the so-called Bellini Cup, a supposedly priceless, jewel-encrusted chalice, from a local museum. So as to maximize our stealth, we even wore ridiculous shoes with three-foot-thick soles made of foam rubber. When, after much effort, we finally deactivated the museum's alarm, Sid, the head thief, stood holding the cup, marveling at its beauty. The rest of us, in celebration of our success, busted out some bubbly, made a toast, drank up, and hurled the glasses against a wall. Sid, who'd drunk straight from the Bellini itself, got so caught up in the moment that he followed suit, smashing the thing to bits. The audience ate it up.

In retrospect, the sketch owed much of its success to our writing and acting, sure, but also to an incredibly funny, rather obscure little film that made me laugh like a woman.

Carl Reiner

I haven't always

been the dapper fashion plate you've come to know

and love. There was a time when, back in the early eighties, I was lucky to own threads that didn't shine like a disco ball. In other words, I was no Huggy Bear.

Actually, I've always been fashion-conscious, but in the days before my career took off, I was a typical starving artist living in New York City, where rent is insanely high. At one point, I hit a major financial snag and was forced to sell everything I owned, including my closetful of slick duds, just to keep the landlord off my ass.

After a while, I'd had enough of just scraping by and decided to make a new start. So I moved out to Los Angeles, where my brother Keenan was earning a pretty good living. "Come on," he declared one night, "we're going to a club." Keenan was always trying to cheer me up. But I was in no mood to get jiggy wid it. Besides, I whined, I had

nothing to wear. "Doesn't matter," he said. "Just put something on, anything." So I draped myself in some nappy-looking polyester and, reluctantly, headed out.

We arrived at the club, and after downing a few drinks I began to feel less self-conscious. Fuck this self-pity shit, I thought. It's boogie time! But as I got up to hit the dance floor, Keenan grabbed my arm. "Let's not get carried away, little brother," he whispered. "After all, you look like a bum."

No sooner had my funk returned, than my funk returned.

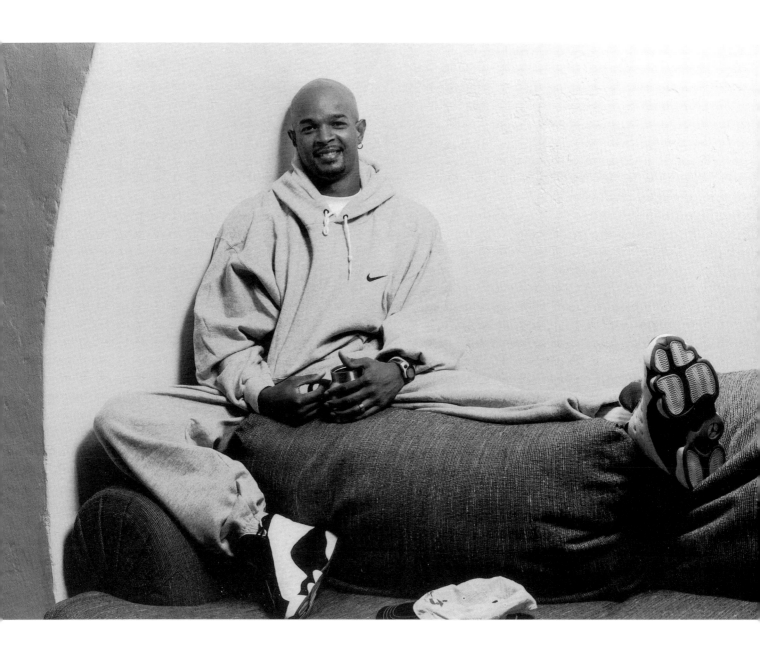

Damon Wayans

My first wife,

Marianne, had a black belt. In bridge.

Upon returning from tournaments she played in around the country, she'd tell me all about them in excruciating detail. If ever a pastime had no need for color commentary, bridge was it. That's nice, I'd say, wilting. I just wasn't the least bit interested. (Golf widows, I feel your pain.)

One weekend, we were invited to her friend's home in Pasadena. All my wife's bridge cronies would be there with their husbands, and she insisted that I accompany her. Great. Another chunk of my life shot to hell. These people were such geeks, they hadn't even heard of Carol Burnett, much less me. But no amount of protesting would help, I knew. So, begrudgingly, I went along.

It was a posh function at a gorgeous home. But I'd attended enough of these events to realize that tedium levels could become toxic. And may I say this one buried the needle. No matter where I turned, all discourse revolved around bridge. Looking back, it's a wonder we spouses didn't commit mass suicide.

Dying of boredom, I excused myself and wandered into the bathroom to splash my face with cold water and rummage through the medicine cabinet for smelling salts. No salts, but I did find a jar of Vaseline and a box of wooden Q-Tips. The wheels began to turn.

In a last-ditch effort to preserve my sanity, I daubed my face with petroleum jelly, snapped some Q-Tips in half, and affixed them to the goo. Then I strode casually back to the epicenter of dullness, where the bridge confabs were at full tilt.

Suddenly, dead silence. All eyes were
upon me.

"Oh, this." I calmly pointed to my cactuslike
countenance. "The Q-Tips box exploded."

Marianne and I were divorced shortly
thereafter.

Tim Conway

As ski slopes go,
the ones in Wisconsin aren't exactly world-class

black diamonds. But when you're a beginner, even the slightest bump is cause for panic.

When I was nineteen and fearless, I decided to brave these vast highlands of the Midwest. I'd been raised in Chicago, and this looked like fearsome terrain indeed. At the time, I had a few ski lessons under my belt, so my technique, crude though it was, was the least of my worries. It was the mere thought of getting on and off the lift that really freaked me out. As any skier will tell you, it's an acquired skill that requires timing and dexterity. Though when it came to skiing, I possessed neither.

I boarded at the base without incident— heart thumping, palms sweating—and as the lift carried me slowly upward, I tried to enjoy the beauty of my surroundings . . . snow-covered pines, tranquil silence. But I just couldn't. Like a gymnast visualizing her routine, I focused on my eventual dismount at the peak. Gotta stick the landing, gotta stick the landing, I told myself over and over. If I didn't, I'd look like a fool. And when you're nineteen, that's worse than death.

As the summit neared, I felt a rush of adrenaline and focused even more intensely. But as I reached the plateau, I was so

determined not to fall on my ass that I stayed aboard a bit longer than I should have. By the time I slid off, the lift had already begun to decline. I must have paused there a second too long, because I felt a nudge from the chair behind me. That was all it took. Soon, I was in a wild downward spiral, plummeting toward the base at Mach 3, hair on fire, trying desperately to avoid maiming anyone, including myself, along the way.

As I neared the bottom of the slope, about fifty yards away, I spotted a small mound of snow, probably placed there specifically for mishaps such as this. But I was going so fast, it barely served as a speed bump, slowing me only slightly just seconds before I crashed, limbs flailing frantically, through a row of skis and into the side of the lodge. Thud! Ouch.

Fortunately, amazingly, bruised ego notwithstanding, I emerged without any serious injuries. Best of all, I was alive! Suddenly, looking foolish seemed trivial. In fact, I was now more determined than ever to conquer that hill. But first, I told myself, I'd perfect the art of stopping. Surely, with the correct technique, that ski lodge wall wouldn't seem nearly as hard.

Nora Dunn

Long ago,

in a place far, far away,
I was mobbed.

And just my luck, not one autograph seeker in the bunch. For you see, I was *mobbed*. As in, The angry mob stormed the castle.

Dateline: Tokyo—I, my wife, Jayne, and our boy, Bill, were touring the town in a limo when we ran smack dab into a bloody revolution. Okay, I admit, it was more of a demonstration. And, come to think of it, it wasn't really all that bloody, either. In fact, not at all. But it *could* have been bloody had the car *actually* run into it. Which it didn't, thank heaven. Oh, the exquisite hypotheses!

As it was, this rowdy assemblage was comprised mainly of red bandanna–wearing, sign-toting, hate-spewing Japanese students who were in the midst of staging a vehement anti-American rally. And just in time for the Allen Family visit. How quaint. They seemed to peer right through our tinted windows. And they were shouting to the rhythm of a big drum, "Yan-kee, go home! Yan-kee, go home!"

But aside from the fact that we were being held hostage in a foreign land, what else was there to worry about, really? After all, the car was equipped with a wet bar. On the other hand, six-year-old Bill, still a teetotaler, was quite alarmed by the spectacle, as any similarly stranded child would be. So, as any similarly stranded child would do, he rolled down a window, stuck his head out, and, in perfect sync with the drumbeat, tried to placate the horde. "We're go-ing home Thurs-day! We're go-ing home Thurs-day!" he chanted.

Intrepid youth? Perhaps. Then again, maybe he just took his dad's comedic counsel too literally: It's all in the timing, son. It's all in the timing.

Steve Allen

My father

is one of the funniest people
I've ever known.

A natural. "David," he once told me, "there's humor everywhere. You just have to look for it." And so I did. *Everywhere.*

Shortly after I'd received this advice, we attended the funeral of my Aunt Sarah. Now, I was just a kid, and kids really don't know how to act or react when they're plopped in the midst of weepy mourners and a stiff. Kids also don't know there are certain things adults will say to put a positive spin on an otherwise morose occasion. My aunt's friends were particularly fond of the meaningless phrase, "She looks like herself." That's what they said as they peered into Aunt Sarah's coffin, "She looks like herself." What the hell were they talking about? "Of course she looks like herself!" I blurted. "What? Do you think Aunt Sarah dies and suddenly looks like Uncle Joe?" Well, it was true, and they knew it.

As much as they all tried to maintain an air of solemnity, everyone eventually broke down and laughed. Everyone, that is, except my father, who took me aside and sternly dispensed another morsel of wisdom, one that totally contradicted the first: "There is a *time* and a *place* for humor," he admonished. Maybe so. But still, I'd knocked 'em, ah, dead.

David Brenner

Never underestimate

the comedic power of personal crisis,

that's my motto. "Take my wife, please," that's my line. Which came to me in a moment of personal crisis. Which made me very famous. Which taught me never to underestimate the comedic power of personal crisis.

In the early days, I used to be a regular on Kate Smith's weekly radio show. It was great exposure, and I took the job very seriously; I was always prepared. Almost always. One afternoon I became nervous and flustered because my writers were late. I was about to go on the air, and I needed material. And, to make matters worse, as I scrambled frantically to get my act together, in walked my wife. With eight of her lady friends! Of all days, she had to pick *now* to pay me a visit. I was on the verge of panic here. But yentas or no yentas, I thought, the show must go on.

Still, I just wanted them out of the room and into the audience. So, exasperated, I begged one of the ushers, "Take my wife, *please*!" Big yucks from the peanut gallery. My wife even broke up. I did, too.

Wish I got paid every time someone used that line. But if it makes people laugh, I guess that's payment enough. Though I'm sure my agent would disagree.

Henny Youngman